# I Met the Virgin Mary in Lourdes

ISBN 979-8-89243-606-9 (paperback)
ISBN 979-8-89428-725-6 (hardcover)
ISBN 979-8-89243-607-6 (digital)

Copyright © 2024 by Valoree Althoff

All rights reserved. No part of this publication may be reproduced, distributed, or transmitted in any form or by any means, including photocopying, recording, or other electronic or mechanical methods without the prior written permission of the publisher. For permission requests, solicit the publisher via the address below.

Christian Faith Publishing
832 Park Avenue
Meadville, PA 16335
www.christianfaithpublishing.com

Printed in the United States of America

# I Met the Virgin Mary in Lourdes

Valoree Althoff

My name is Bernadette. I live in Lourdes, France. It is hard growing up here. We have little money, and I have eight brothers and sisters, but I am happy, even though I am sick a lot.

I like to walk and explore by the river. The river is peaceful. One day, my sister and I searched for firewood by the river. My sister went ahead of me because I wanted to find a better place to cross the river so I would not get my socks wet. It is so easy for me to get a cold. I felt a large gust of wind, but nothing moved, so I turned around to see where it was coming from. Behind me in the grotto was a sparkling figure wearing a white dress, blue sash, and white veil. I had to go closer.

The sparkling white figure was a lady. Her smile gave me a sense of peace. She made the sign of the cross while holding her ivory and gold rosary. I took out my rosary, kneeled, and prayed with her. I visited her three days later, and she asked me to come back. Day after day, I returned to talk to the beautiful lady in white. Sometimes my sisters or friends would come with me, but no one else saw her.

I returned to the grotto by the river a total of eighteen times. On one visit, the lady told me to drink from the water and eat the herb where she pointed, to forgive my sins. I was confused because she pointed to a wet spot of dirt.

When I dug up the dirt, I found a spring of water!

Day after day, I asked the beautiful lady in white her name because everyone kept asking who I was seeing. Only a few people believed me. Most of the time, she would respond with a smile. Finally, one day she said to call her the Immaculate Conception.

The lady's name did not mean much to me, but my priest at church understood. He said that the beautiful lady I was speaking to, my friend, was the Virgin Mary, Mother of Jesus. I was confused. Why would she visit me?

I visited the lady a few more times, but then she stopped appearing. Her last request was to build a church nearby. It took some time, but you can visit the church. The church is on a hill overlooking the river.

After years of asking me questions, people believe me now. The church confirmed the water from the spring had healed seventy people. Many more people think the water cured them too.

As I grow older, I do not like the attention. I decided to become a nun to serve the church.

I never really understood why I was chosen by Mother Mary to share her message. I tell people, "The Virgin used me as a broom to remove the dust. When the work is done, the broom is put behind the door again." Mother Mary told me, "She does not promise to make me happy in this world, but in the next." I will forever remember the time I spent with the beautiful lady, the Immaculate Conception.

# Story of Saint Bernadette

Bernadette Soubirous was born in Lourdes, France, on January 7, 1844, the oldest of nine children. As a child, Bernadette contracted cholera and lived the rest of her life with severe chronic asthma.

Thursday, February 11, 1858: The first apparition; Bernadette was fourteen.

February 25, 1858: Bernadette drank from the spring in penance.

March 2, 1858: The lady asked for the chapel to be built.

March 25, 1858: Bernadette asked the lady her name, and she finally replied, "I am the Immaculate Conception."

In 1862, the Church authorities and the French government confirmed Bernadette spoke the truth of the apparitions. Bernadette did not like the attention, so she went to a school run by the Sisters of Charity of Nevers, France. She officially joined the religious habit on July 29, 1866, and became Sister Marie-Bernarde.

The church that Mary requested, the Basilica of the Immaculate Conception, was built in 1876. Its crypt under the basilica was the first church and was completed in 1866. Bernadette was not present for the consecration, but her father participated in the construction and was present at the opening on Pentecost Sunday. The Upper Basilica was constructed on top of it.

Bernadette contracted tuberculosis and died at age thirty-five on April 16, 1879, while praying the rosary. Her final words were, "Blessed Mary, Mother of God, pray for me. A poor sinner, a poor sinner." She was laid to rest in Saint Gildard Convent, and her incorruptible body has been visited there since August 3, 1925.

Her body was exhumed three times. The first time was September 22, 1909, and she was found with a rosary and crucifix, both oxidized, but she was incorrupt.

Bernadette was beatified in 1925 and canonized by Pius XI on December 8, 1933, on the Feast of the Immaculate Conception. Saint Bernadette's feast day is April 16.

# About the Author

Valoree Althoff took her first Catholic pilgrimage to Italy and France in 2012. In 2023, she took her second pilgrimage to Ireland, where she and her mother were able to visit the Knox shrine. Valoree has served as a lecturer at Saint Mary's Parish in Farmington, New Mexico, since 2010. Her faith has been deepened through books and her pilgrimages. Valoree has been married to Andy Althoff since 2009. She spends her time as a dental hygienist, serving organizations as a parliamentarian, and at home with her fur babies.

Printed in the USA
CPSIA information can be obtained
at www.ICGtesting.com
LVHW071540071224
798393LV00013B/107